Maltese for foreigners: 700+ everyday words and expressions to learn Maltese
by Alain de Raymond

© Alain de Raymond, 2017

All rights reserved

To my parents. And my friends in Malta.

Table of Contents

Introduction 9
1. Pronunciation 11
2. Greeting 13
3. Essential sentences about Maltese 15
4. Essential expressions and words 17
5. Non-essential filling words 19
6. Connecting words 21
7. How questions start 23
   7.1 Sentences with kemm: 23
   7.2 Sentences with xi: 24
   7.3 Xi, some, all and none 25
8. The prepositions and pronouns: making sense of Maltese 27
   8.1 - words: prepositions 27
   8.2 The crucial placing of pronouns 28
   8.3 Għal: expressions and pronouns 29
   8.4 Ta': expressions and pronouns 30
   8.5 Minn: expressions and pronouns 30
   8.6 Bi: expressions and pronouns 31
   8.7 Ma': expressions and pronouns 32
   8.8 Bħal: expressions and pronouns 33
   8.9 Fi: expressions and pronouns 34
   8.10 Sa': expressions 35
   8.11 Demonstrative pronouns 35
   8.12 To have: with għand 36
   8.13 Negative: expressions with mhux 36
9. Places and directions 39
   9.1 Here and there 39
   9.2 Where is… 39
   9.3 Directions 41
10. The most used verbs 43

11. Adjectives: antonyms 47
12. Everyday Maltese words 51
   12.1 Fill in a form 51
   12.2 Weather 51
   12.3 At the doctor 52
   12.4 Money & at the shop 52
   12.5 Home..54
   12.6: Restaurant 55
   12.7 Transport...56
   12.8 Time 57

13. Extra useful phrases 59
   13.1 On the phone..59
   13.2 Compliments 59
   13.3 Party at friend's place 60
   13.4 Others 60

14. Fun extras 63

15. Learn more Maltese 65

16. The final word – About the author 67

Introduction

Hi!

Understanding Maltese can be challenging. The Maltese you read is not the same as the one you hear. Prepositions and pronouns are not like in other European languages. Add to that many expressions, and you get the picture.

The purpose of this book is to cover the most **spoken Maltese** possible, and the least grammar. We'll focus on the most used words and expressions Maltese use in their everyday lives.

First, we'll learn how to **pronounce** in Maltese, followed by a chapter about **greeting** and some **essential sentences** to use like 'please repeat'. Maltese use many **non-essential words** to fill up their sentences, which is in the next chapter.

Second, we'll focus on **connecting words** like 'if', 'about' and 'because', followed by a chapter on **interrogative pronouns** like 'how' and 'when'.

Third, we'll see how **prepositions** (for, in, to…) can help us to understand the meaning of a sentence with a little grammar but also many expressions. Next subject is how to use the **attached pronouns** (you, him,…).

Fourth, small **directions** will be dealt with. You'll learn to ask questions like 'Where's the post office?' and subsequently, we'll see which are the most common **verb** conjugations. A number of **antonyms** will be added, so you can learn them in pairs.

We'll finish with **everyday words and phrases** in particular situations, like on the phone, in the shop and compliments.

When we see new words, the structure is for example:

- **L-għodwa t-tajba**: good morning (*the morning the good*). Polite way.
- **Maltese words**: translation (*literal translation*). Extra information.

The literal translation is added because some translations don't make much sense.

Some words may have the female and plural form added, usually -a and -in:

- **Sinjur**, -a, -i: rich.

All Maltese words in bold can be heard through a link to a **recording** at the end of the lists. All recordings are available on one page on: goo.gl/5zEYjt.

Happy learning,

Alain

1. Pronunciation

Let's start with how to pronounce Maltese with the alphabet. It is very similar to the English alphabet. The bold letters have a different or special pronunciation.

Aa Bb Ċċ Dd Ee Ff Ġġ Gg Għgħ Hh Ħħ Ii Ieie Jj Kk Ll Mm Nn Oo Pp Qq Rr Ss Tt Uu Vv Ww Xx Żż Zz

- Ċċ: like **ch**eck
- Ġġ: like **G**eorge
- Gg: like **g**reat
- Għgħ: unpronounced, in Maltese "għajn"
- Hh: unpronounced, in Maltese "akka", unless it is at the end of a word, then it is pronounced like ħ
- Ħħ: like **h**ard, but a little harder
- Ii: like **f**ear
- Ieie: longer than i
- Jj: like **y**ounger
- Qq: like ()archer, the sound before archer but a little harder
- Uu: like **y**ou
- Xx: like **sh**ort
- Żż: like **z**oo
- Zz: like **ts**unami

The għ does influence the pronunciation of other letters. If before an 'i', as in 'ngħid' (I tell), the għi is pronounced like the i in pride. If it is written at the end of a word, it takes the 'ħ' sound. However, it is unpronounced when it is hidden. In that case, the għ is written like ' as in nista' (I can).

11

Note that there is no c in the Maltese alphabet, only ċ. The 'u' changes into a 'w' if the word before ends with a vowel. Two vowels never follow each other directly in a word. Between words, they are avoided but it can still happen.

Watch out when you're looking for a word in the dictionary. For example, when you're looking for a word starting with għ, don't look for it at the letter g.

2. Greeting

Let's see how to greet in Maltese.

- **Aw**: hi. Very informal.
- **Ħellow**: hello. Sometimes written in other ways.

- **L-għodwa t-tajba**: good morning (*the morning the good*). Polite way.
- **Bonġu**: hello. Only used in the morning.
- **Bonswa**: good evening.
- **Il-waranofsinhar it-tajjeb**: good afternoon (*the after-half-day the good*).
- **Il-lejl it-tajjeb**: good night (*the night the good*).
- **Kif inti**: how are you.
- **Kif aħna**: how are you (*how are we*).

- **Mhux ħażin**: not bad (*it is not bad*).
- **Tajjeb**: good.

- **Ċaw**: goodbye.
- **Il-ġurnata t-tajba**: have a nice day (*the day the good*).
- **Narak**: see you.
- **Saħħa**: bye (*health*).

14

3. Essential sentences about Maltese

Questions foreigners can ask:
- **Xi tfisser**…: what does … mean? (*what she means*).
- **Kif tgħid … bil-Malti**? How do you say … in Maltese? (*how you say… with Maltese*).
- **Titkellem bil-Malti**?: Do you speak Maltese? (*you speak with Maltese*).
- **Erġa għidli**: repeat (*repeat tell me*).

Other sentences to introduce questions:
- **Ma smajtekx**: I didn't hear you.
- **Skużani**: excuse me.
- **Għandi mistoqsija**: I have a question.

Other sentences for beginners:
- **Ma nafx**: I don't know.
- **Jiena barrani**: I am a foreigner (*I foreigner*).
- **Jiena barranija** I am a foreigner (*I foreigner*).
- **Aħna barranin** we are foreigners (*we foreigners*).
- **Qed nitgħallem Malti**: I'm learning Maltese.
- **Għandi tweġiba**: I have an answer.

Extra words:
- **Żball**, -ji : mistake.
- **Kors**: course.
- **Tikka**: dot.
- **Kors tal-Malti**: Maltese course (*course of the Maltese*).
- **Għalliem**, -a, -a: the teacher.

- **Kelma**, kelmiet/kliem: word.
- **Lingwa**: language.
- **Ilsien**: language.
- **Risposta**: response, answer.

4. Essential expressions and words

Some words often come back in Maltese. The following ones a foreigner should be able to use them in everyday language:

- **Iva**: yes. Sometimes pronounced iwa.
- **Le**: no.
- **Jew**: or.
- **Eżatt**: exact, right.
- **Tassew**: really.
- **Issa**: now. Often used in front of sentences.
- **Isma'**: listen. Also often used in front of sentences.
- **Grazzi**: thanks.
- **Ħafna**: a lot, much/many.
- **Grazzi ħafna**: thanks a lot.
- **Ftit**: a little, little.
- **Veru / vera**: true.
- **Diġa**: already, shortened as **ġa**.
- **Stess**: same, self. Often used as **l-istess** (*the same*).

The following ones are adverbs and constructions with verbs:

- **Jekk jogħġbok**: please (*if it pleases you*). Shortened as jj.
- **Jekk jogħġobkom**: please (*if it pleases you*). In the plural.
- **Jiddispjaċini**: I'm sorry (*it sorries me*).
- **Ejja**: go, come on!
- **Jaqaw**: possibly.

- **Suppost**: supposedly, supposed.
- **Ovvjament**: obviously. Shortened as '**ovvja**.'

5. Non-essential filling words

Some frequently used words don't mean much. They are used to fill sentences. So make sure to understand them. Use them to sound Maltese.

The following are usually used at the beginning of the sentences:

- **Imma**: but.
- **Uwejja**: come on, it isn't possible, are you joking.
- **U imbagħad**: well, later. Sometimes without u.
- **Ara**: look.
- **Miskin, -a**: poor thing (*pathetic*).
- **Ħa nigħdlek**: I'm telling you (*it took I tell you*).
- **Ifhem**: understand.
- **Wara kollox**: after all.
- **Insomma**: maybe, a little, well.
- **Żgur**: sure.
- **Dażgur**: sure. But a little stronger.

The following ones are used everywhere in sentences:

- **Mela**: well. Usually the first word foreigners learn.
- **Jiġifieri**: I mean (*it means to me*).
- **Kif ukoll**: as well as, and (*how also*).
- **Allura**: then.
- **Anzi**: indeed, rather.
- **Qed ngħid**: I'm saying.

Those are used at the end of the sentences:
- **Ta**. Means nothing.
- **Ux**: right?
- **Jew**? right? (*or*).
- **Hi**: mate, 'bro.'

These ones sometimes stand alone:
- **Ajma**: ouch, it hurts.
- **Kif**: what? (*how*).
- **U le**: that can't be right (*and no*).
- **Illalu**: wow!
- **Orrajt**: all right.

6. Connecting words

Many sentences will start with the following words. So it's a good start to already know the first.

- **Dwar**: about. Also used as **madwar**.
- **Anki / anke**: also.
- **Ukoll / wkoll**: also. The u turns into a w if the previous word ends with a vowel.
- **Lilek ukoll**: same to you (*to you also*).
- **U**: and.
- **Waqt**: while, during.
- **Dalwaqt**: soon.
- **Filwaqt li**: as, while (*in-while that*).
- **Minħabba**: because.
- **Għax**: because, as a result of.
- **Peress li**: because of.
- **Li**: that. Used as connection word, not a way to indicate something.
- **Biss**: only.
- **Biex**: in order to.
- **Sabiex**: in order to.
- **Iżda**: but, however.
- **Bla**: without.
- **Mingħajr**: without.
- **Basta**: if, on the condition that.
- **Kieku**: if, on the condition that.
- **Jekk**: if.
- **Minflok**: instead of. '
- **Flok**: instead of.

21

- **Skont**: according to.
- **Sadanittant**: meanwhile.

One combination often used:
- **Jekk trid**: if you want.

7. How questions start

In Maltese, questions start with the interrogative pronouns like most languages. We'll see some expressions and phrases with kemm and xi too in this chapter.

- **Min**: who.
- **Fejn**: where.
- **Meta**: when.
- **Kif**: how.
- **Kemm**: how much.
- **X'**: what.
- **Għaliex**: why, because.
- **Għalfejn**: why.
- **Liema**: which.

7.1 Sentences with kemm:

Kemm in itself is just like in English used when asking for a price. When starting a sentence, it can have two meanings. With questions, it means 'how much' or 'how many'. And in other sentences, it's used to say 'so much', 'so' or 'such'. For instance:

- **Kemm inti kbir!**: You're so big! (*how much you are big*).

- **Kemm għandek nadif!**: your place is so clean (*how much you have clean*).
- **Kemm inti basla!**: You are such an idiot! (*how much you are onion*).
- **Kemm għandek żmien?**: How old are you? (*how much do you have time*).

Other combinations:
- **Sakemm**: until, unless.
- **Tant kemm**: so much.
- **Tant**: so much.

7.2 Sentences with xi:

Xi is sometimes shortened x'. Don't confuse xi with the -x at the end of verbs. That is used for the negative.

Xi has a few meanings: 'what', 'some' and 'more or less.' Xi as in 'more or less' is used with numbers. Let's see some sentences using the first meaning, 'what'.

If it stands on its own, it is:
- **Xiex**: what?

- **Xi trid**: what do you want? Rather direct question.
- **X'inhu**: what is it?
- **X'inhi**: what is it?
- **X'ġara?**: what happened?
- **X'sar?**: what happened?
- **X'għamilt?**: What did I/you do?
- **X'waħda din?** What's this (*what one this*)? To use when you're surprised.
- **Taf x'naf**: you know what I know.
- **Xi dwejjaq**: how sad (*what narrow*).
- **X'taħseb?**: what do you think?

7.3 Xi, some, all and none

Let's see some words with xi as 'some'. They are similar to those with 'all' and 'none.' All is used with:
- **Kull**: every, each.

- **Ħadd**: no one.
- **Xi ħadd**: someone.
- **Kulħadd**: everyone.

- **Mkien**: nowhere, place.
- **Xi mkien**: somewhere.
- **Kullimkien**: everywhere (*every place*).
- **Flimkien**: together (*in place*).

- **Xi kultant**: sometimes. Also without xi.
- **Ħaġa**: thing.
- **Xi ħaġa**: something.

Some other words and expressions with every and no:
- **Xejn**: nothing.
- **Kollox**: everything.
- **Qatt**: never.
- **Spiss**: often.
- **Dejjem**: always.
- **Kuljum**: every day.
- **Kull wieħed**: every single one (*every one*).
- **Kollu** (male), **kollha** (female), **kollhom** (plural): all, whole.
- **Sħiħ**, -a, sħaħ: whole, entire.

25

- **Xulxin**: each other.
- **Lanqas xejn**: I don't like it at all (*not even nothing*).
- **Lanqas**: not even.

8. The prepositions and pronouns: making sense of Maltese

Because of the Arabic influences on Maltese, many beginning students have difficulties making sense out of the Maltese sentences. If you don't know enough words, you won't know the meaning of the sentence. Which word belongs to which word?

8.1 - words: prepositions

An important step to learn Maltese is to start understanding the - words, or prepositions. Those words usually use a - just after them, and sometimes a '. Let's see the main ones:

- **il-**: the article. Just translate it as 'the'. If the noun starts with s, ċ, d, n, r, s, t, x, z, or ż, the l is replaced by the first letter of the noun.
- **Bi**: with (objects). With the article, it becomes **bil-**. And without **b'**.
- **Fi**: in. With article **fil-** and without **f'**.
- **Bħal**: like. With article **bħall-** without **bħal**.
- **Għal**: for, to. With article **għall-**, without **għal**.
- **Lil**: to. With article **lill-**, without **lil**.
- **Sa**: until. With article **sal-**, without **s'**.
- **Ta'**: of. With article **tal-**, without **ta'**.
- **Ma'**: with (persons). With article **mal-**, without **ma'**.
- **Minn**: from. With article **mill-**, without **minn**.

So whenever Maltese want to say with, of, from or in, they'll use words with a -. Which is very, very often. So even though you might not understand the vocabulary of the following sentence, you can already know a few things:

Il-missier mar mat-tabib fil-kamra tas-sodda.

<u>The</u> 'unknown noun' 'other word' <u>with the</u> 'unknown word' <u>in the</u> 'unknown noun' <u>of the</u> 'unknown noun'.

Recognising and understanding the - nouns, or prepositions, will greatly help understanding the language. You can practice on many news websites to get used to these words.

One last point. Lil is not the same as li. **Li** is also frequently used. It's not a prepositions and means that. So it connects many Maltese sentences.

8.2 The crucial placing of pronouns

Another important challenge for Maltese students not acquainted with the Arabic languages, are the pronouns. Unlike most European languages, these pronouns are attached to the previous word. For example:

- Mingħajrek: without you.
- Mingħajr: without.
- -ek: you.

So if a word ends with -k, you may already suspect it has the pronoun 'you'. So the attached pronouns are:

- **-ni, -i, -ja**: me
- **-ek, -ok, -k**: you
- **-u, -h**: him
- **-ha**: her
- **-na**: us
- **-kom**: you
- **-hom**: them

An example: darhom: their house. Or rasi: my head.

Now, let's see expressions with the prepositions and add the pronouns to them.

8.3 Għal: expressions and pronouns

- **Għalxejn**: for nothing, for no reason.
- **Għaliex**: why, because.
- **Għalfejn**: why.
- **Għal-bejgħ**: for sale.
- **Għalkemm**: although.
- **Għalhekk**: that is why, therefore (*for there*).
- **Għal xiex**: for what, why.
- **Għalkollox**: totally.
- **Totalment**: totally.

- **Għalija**: for me.
- **Għalik**: for you.
- **Għalih**: for him.
- **Għaliha**: for her.
- **Għalina**: for us.
- **Għalikom**: for you.
- **Għalihom**: for them.

Note that lil- is also used as 'for' or 'to': lili, lilek, lilu, lilha, lilna, lilkom, lilhom: (to me, you,…). It is very similar to għal-.

8.4 Ta': expressions and pronouns
- **Ta'xejn**: you're welcome (*of nothing*).
- **Ta'jdejna**: affordable for us (*of our hands*).
- **Ta'vera**: truly, true (*of truth*).

Ta' is also used with shops that sell a category of food. For example, laħam means meat. **Tal-laħam** is the butcher (of the meat).
- **Tiegħi**: my.
- **Tiegħek**: your.
- **Tiegħu**: his.
- **Tagħha**: her.
- **Tagħna**: our.
- **Tagħkom**: your.
- **Tagħhom**: their.

8.5 Minn: expressions and pronouns
Don't confuse minn (from) having a double n with min (who) using a single n. Sometimes, **mingħand** is used but it means the same as minn. Many of the Maltese expressions somehow make sense if you compare the literal translation and the meaning. For example the first expression:
- **Minbarra**: except (*outside from*).
- **Mill-ewwel**: at once (*from first*).
- **Mill-inqas**: at least (*from least*).
- **Mill-qrib**: closely (*from a close place*).
- **Barra minn hekk**: moreover (*outside from like that*).
- **Mill-ġdid**: again (*from new*).

- **Mill-kbar**: enormous (*from the biggest*).
- **Ftit minn kollox**: a bit from everything.
- **X'minnek**: long time I haven't seen you (*what from you*).

- **Minni**: from me.
- **Minnek**: from you.
- **Minnu**: from him.
- **Minnha**: from her.
- **Minna**: from us.
- **Minnkom**: from you.
- **Minnhom**: from them.

8.6 Bi: expressions and pronouns
- **B'xejn**: free (*with nothing*).
- **B'kollox**: altogether (*with everything*).
- **B'ħafna**: with a lot of.
- **B'hekk**: thus (*with like that*).
- **B'mod**: in … way. Used with adjective, e.g.: **b'mod**

  uffiċjali: In an official way.

- **Bil-mod**: slowly (*with manner*).
- **Bil-Malti**: in Maltese (*with Maltese*).
- **Bl-Ingliż**: in English (*with English*).
- **Grazzi bil-quddiem**: thanks in advance (*thanks with in front of*).
- **Bis-serjetà**: seriously (*with seriousness*).
- **Bil-qalb**: warmly (*with heart*). Warmly in the figurative way, 'with a warm heart'.

- **Bil-mixi**: by foot (*with walking*).
- **Bil-kwiet**: silently (*with silence*).

- **Bilkemm**: hardly, almost.
- **Bilfors**: compulsory, by force.
- **Bilqiegħda**: seated, seating (*with she stays*).
- **Poġġi bilqiegħda**: be seated (*put with she stays*).

- **Bija**: with me.
- **Bik**: with you.
- **Bih**: with him.
- **Biha**: with her.
- **Bina**: with us.
- **Bikom**: with you.
- **Bihom**: with them.

An expression with the pronoun:
- **Merħba bik**: welcome (*welcome with you*).

Note that the pronouns with ma' are used more frequently than those with bi.

8.7 Ma': expressions and pronouns

Do not confuse ma' -with a '- with the ma from the negative, which does not have a '. The ma stands just in front of a verb, and an 'x' will usually be added to the verb:
- ma naħdimx: I don't work.

- **Matul**: during (*with the length*).

- **Miegħi**: with me.
- **Miegħek**: with you.
- **Miegħu**: with him.
- **Magħha**: with her.
- **Magħna**: with us.
- **Magħkom**: with you.
- **Magħhom**: with them.

An expression with the pronoun:
- **Ejja miegħi**: come with me.

8.8 Bħal: expressions and pronouns

Bħal has a few meanings: like, as, in the capacity of.
- **Bħalissa**: now, at the present time (*like now*).

- **Bħali**: like me.
- **Bħalek**: like you.
- **Bħalu**: like him.
- **Bħalha**: like her.
- **Bħalna**: like us.
- **Bħalkom**: like you.
- **Bħalhom**: like them.

An expression with the pronoun:
- **Bħal xiex?**: like what?
- **M'hawnx bħalek**: there's no one like you.

Qis- can be used instead of bħal. For example 'like them' you can use both:

- qishom and
- bħalhom.

8.9 Fi: expressions and pronouns

- **F'kaz ta'**: in case of. Sometimes with li instead of ta'.
- **F'nofs**: in the middle of (*in half*).
- **F'idejk**: in your hands. Meaning in your control, it's your responsibility now. Note the -k at the end of the hands.
- **F'kelma waħda**: in short (*in word one*).
- **F'liema sens**: how exactly (*in which sense*).

- **Filgħodu**: in the morning.
- **Filgħaxija**: in the evening.

- **Fil-bżonn**: in need.
- **Fis-sens**: in the sense.
- **Fil-ħin**: on time (*in the time*).
- **Fil-fatt**: in fact.
- **Fiex nista' naqdik?**: how can I help you (in what I can I help you). Also:
- **Kif nista' naqdik?**: how can I help you (how I can I help you).
- **Fl-istess ħin**: at the same time (*in the same time*).
- **Fl-aħħar**: finally (*in the last*).
- **Fl-aħħar minuta**: at the last moment (*in the last minute*).

- **Fija**: in me.
- **Fik**: in you.
- **Fiħ**: in him.
- **Fiha**: in her.
- **Fina**: in us.
- **Fikom**: in you.
- **Fihom**: in them.

Sometimes, ġo is used instead of fi.

8.10 Sa': expressions

Sa means until.

- **Mimli sax-xifer**: completely full (full until the edge).
- **Sa issa**: until now.

8.11 Demonstrative pronouns

Sometimes, demonstrative pronouns will be connected with a - as well:

- **Dal-ħin**: that time.

So the demonstrative pronouns are (male, female, plural):

- **Dan, din, dawn**: this, these.
- **Dak, dik, dawk**: that, those.

One expression:

- **Tajba din**: that's a good one! (*good this*).

8.12 To have: with għand

The verb 'to have' uses the attached pronouns to conjugate the verb:

- **Għandi** (I have)
- **Għandek** (you have)
- **Għandu** (he has)
- **Għandha** (she has)
- **Għandna** (we have)
- **Għandkom** (you have)
- **Għandhom** (they have)

Some expressions with to have:

- **Għandi x'nagħmel**: I'm busy (*I have what I do*).
- **Għandi bżonn**: I need (*I have need*).
- **Għandi pjaċir**: nice to meet you (*I have pleasure*).
- **M'għandekx x'tagħmel**: Aren't you busy? (*you don't have what you do*).
- **M'għandekx raġun**: you're not right (*you don't have reason*).
- **Għandi ċans**: I have a chance.

8.13 Negative: expressions with mhux

Verbs in the negative add a ma or m' at the beginning and -x at the end. So it is for hu (he is): mhux (it is not). It is very often used, as with the following expressions:

- **Tgħid mhux hekk**: don't tell me that's true (*you tell me it is not like that*).
- **Mhux ta' b'xejn**: no wonder (*it is not of with nothing*).
- **Mhux hekk**: it's not like that.

- **Mhux problema**: no problem (*it is not problem*).
- **Mhux vera/veru**: it isn't true.
- **Mhux minnhu**: it isn't true (*it is not from it*).

9. Places and directions

Malta is a rather small island. So asking for directions could be a bit strange. However, small directions are common. So let's learn how to ask for directions, plus essential words to give those directions.

9.1 Here and there

- **Hawn**: here.
- **Hemm**: there.
- **Hekk**: like that.
- **Hekk hu**: that's how it is (*like that it is*).
- **Hawnhekk**: right here (*here like that*).
- **Hemmhekk**: right there (*there like that*).

Some expressions with hawn and hemm:

- **M'hemmx imniex**: you're welcome (*there is not I am not*).
- **M'hemmx x'tagħmel**: there's nothing you can do (*there is not what you do*).
- **M'hawnx itjeb**: heaven on a plate (*there is not better*).
- **X'hemm ġdid?**: What's new? (*what there new?*).
- **M'hemmx għalfejn**: there is no need (*there is not why*).
- **Min hemm?**: Who's there?
- **Ħudni hemm**: take me there.
- **Ara min hawn**: look who's here.

9.2 Where is...

- **Fejn hu/hi...**: Where is...
- **Kif nasal sa...**: How do I arrive at...

- **Nixtieg nara...**: I would like to see (*I would like I see*).
- **Irrid immur...**: I want to go... (*I want I go*).

- **Ajruport**: airport.
- **Lukanda**: hotel. You can also just say hotel.
- **Triq**: the street.
- **Port**: seaport.
- **Bini**: building.
- **Knisja**: church.
- **Pulizija**: police.
- **Teatru**: theatre.
- **Palazz**: place.
- **Festa**: feast, holiday.
- **Pjazza**: square.
- **Sptar**: hospital.
- **Ristorant**: restaurant.
- **Suq**: market.
- **Garaxx**: garage.
- **Karozza**: car.
- **Skola**: school.
- **Hanut**: shop.
- **Plajja**: beach.
- **Monument**: monument.
- **Mużew**: museum.
- **Veduta**: view.
- **Katidral**: cathedral.
- **Posta**: post office.
- **Post**: place.

9.3 Directions

Some of the words below use the attached pronouns from the previous chapter. Those are indicated. For example:

- fuqek: on you.
- fosthom: between them.

- **Fuq**: above, on. (uses attached pronouns)
- **Isfel**: down, downstairs.
- **Taħt**: below, under. (uses attached pronouns)
- **Qrib**: a place close or nearby. It's a noun. (uses attached pronouns)
- **Ħdejn**: close to, nearby, next to. (uses attached pronouns)
- **Fejn**: where, near. (uses attached pronouns)
- **Bogħod**: far.
- **Fost**: among. (uses attached pronouns)
- **Bejn**: between, among. (uses attached pronouns)
- **Lejn**: towards. (uses attached pronouns)
- **Xellug**: left.
- **Lemin**: right.
- **Dritt**: straight.
- **Qabel**: before. (uses attached pronouns)
- **Wara**: behind, after. (uses attached pronouns)
- **Quddiem**: in front of. (uses attached pronouns)
- **Barra**: outside.
- **Ġewwa**: inside.
- **Kontra**: against.

Useful expressions:
- **S'hemm**: to that place (*until there*).
- **Intlift**: I'm lost.
- **Dur fuq il-lemin**: turn right (*turn on the right*).
- **Dur fuq ix-xellug**: turn left (*turn on the left*).
- **Ejja ħdejja**: come near me.
- **'l bogħod mill-verità**: far from the truth.
- **Wara ftit**: after a while.
- **Kemm bogħod**: how far.

10. The most used verbs

Maltese verbs use the Arabic conjugations. It is beyond the scope of this book to go into detail. Know that the pronouns are only used to stress them.
- Jiena nifhem. I understand (and the others don't).

And if there is no accompanying verb, it means the verb 'to be' has to be used.
- **Jien/jiena**: I am.
- **Int/inti**: you are.
- **Hu/huwa**: he is.
- **Hi/hija**: she is.
- **Aħna**: we are.
- **Intom**: you are.
- **Huma**: they are.

Also note that most verbs are composed of 3 main letters, which are also used to form other Maltese words. See the K, T and B in the example below. They are the 3 main letters.
- Tikteb: you write.
- Nkiteb: it was written.
- Kittiebi: tending to write.
- Kotba: books.
- Ktejjeb: booklet.

There are even more verbs and nouns related to writing with those three letters. Find more detailed explanations about the verbs' grammar in chapter 15. Let's see the most common Maltese conjugations.

Two combinations:
- **Fhimt**?: understood?
- **Nifhem**: I understand.

- **X'jismek?**: What's your name? (*what is name you?*)
- **Jisimni**: my name is (*it is my name*).

In the present tense:
- **Għandna**: we have.
- **Nċempel**: I call.
- **Ċċempel**: you call.
- **Mmorru**: we go.
- **Nixtieg**: I would like
- **Nsir**: I become.
- **Ssir**: it/he becomes.
- **Nikteb**: I write.
- **Tmur**: you go.
- **Nsibu**: we find.
- **Jkolli**: I have to, I must.
- **Jkollu**: he has to, he must.
- **Titkellem**: you speak.
- **Nżomm**: I keep.
- **Tipprova**: you try.
- **Nħoss**: I feel.
- **Tintuża**: you use.
- **Jogħġobni**: I like.
- **Niprefferi**: I prefer.

In the past tense:
- **Qal**: he said.
- **Qalet**: she said.
- **Għamel**: he did.
- **Wasalna**: we arrived.
- **Sar**: he/it became, it took place.
- **Saret**: she became.
- **Ġejt**: I came, you came.
- **Ġie**: he came.
- **Mort**: I went.
- **Kont**: I was, you were.
- **Kien**: he was.
- **Kienet**: she was.
- **Ried**: he wanted.
- **Ħareġ**: he left.
- **Rajt**: you saw.

In the imperative:
- **Ieqaf**: stop!
- **Isma'**: listen.
- **Ftakar**: remember.
- **Idħol**: enter. Or: you may enter.
- **Tinsiex**: don't forget.
- **Tibżax**: don't be afraid.
- **Tinkwetax**: don't worry.

With the future tense:
- **Jista' jkun**: could be.

- **Se jkun**: it will be.
- **Sejjer** (male), **sejra** (female), **sejrin** (plural): for the future tense, to use with another verb in the present tense. It is more simple just to use '**se**'.

With the present continuous:

- **Qed tara**: now you see (*you are seeing*).
- **Qed ngħid**: I am telling, I am saying. Often used in the middle of sentences.
- **Qed**: used to indicate the present continuous, together with another verb. **Qiegħed** (male), **qiegħda** (female) and **qegħdin** (plural) can also be used. These last tree are mostly used when they stand alone. The translation would be 'he/she is staying' or 'he/she is present'. In the plural: they are staying, they are present.

Other expressions:

- **Stenna ftit**: wait a bit.
- **Naħseb li**: I think that.
- **Ma jimpurtax**: It doesn't matter (*it is not important*).
- **Naf x'iġiefiri**: I know what it means.

11. Adjectives: antonyms

A good way to learn adjectives is to learn them by pairs, just like in other languages. Remember that the female normally ends with -a and the plural with -in. Also note that the adjectives are placed behind the nouns:

- Il-kelb kbir: the big dog.

If you forget one of the antonyms, you can also just use mhux:

- mhux kbir: not big

- **Mimli**, -ja, -jin: full.
- **Vojt**, -a, -a: empty.
- **Kbir**, -a, kbar: big.
- **Żgħir**, -a, żgħar: small.
- **Għali**: expensive.
- **Rħis**, -a, rħas: cheap.
- **Għoli**, għolja, għoljin: high, tall.
- **Baxx**, -a, -i: low.
- **Kuntent**, -a, -i: happy.
- **Mdejjaq**, mdejqa, mdejqin: unhappy.
- **Nadif**, -a, ndaf: clean.
- **Maħmuġ**, -a, -in: dirty.
- **Sabiħ**, -a, sbieħ: beautiful.
- **Ikrah**, kerha, koroh: ugly.
- **Żagħżugħ**, -a, żgħażagħ: young.
- **Anzjan**, -a, -i: old, elder. For persons.
- **Antik**, -a, -i: ancient. For objects.
- **Qadim**, -a, qodma: old. For objects.

- **Ġdid**, -a, ġodda: new.
- **Twil**, -a, twal: long, tall.
- **Qasir**, -a, qsar: short.
- **Tqil**, -a, tqal: heavy, difficult.
- **Hafif**, -a, ħfief: light, easy.
- **Fqir**, -a, fqar: poor.
- **Sinjur**, -a, -i: rich.

Some antonyms with expressions:
- **Ewwel**, ewlenija, ewlenin: first.
- **Aħħar**, -ija, -in: last.
- **L-aħħar darba**: last time.
- **Sew**, -wa: well, truth.
- **Kollox sewwa?**: everything ok?
- **Tajjeb**, tajba, tajbin: good.
- **Hazin**, -a, ħzien: bad.

Adjectives from Italian don't adapt to the female and the plural:
- **Diffiċli**: difficult.
- **Faċli**: easy.
- **Possibli**: possible.
- **Impossibbli**: impossible.

Adverbs:
- **Fortunament**: fortunately.
- **Sfortunament**: unfortunately.
- **Bil-mod**: slowly (*with manner*).
- **Malajr**: quick.

And some other antonyms:
- **Bidu**: the start, the beginning.
- **Tmiem**: the end.
- **Tard**: late.
- **Kmieni**: early.
- **Iktar tard**: later (*more late*).
- **Iktar kmieni**: earlier (*more early*).
- **Aħjar**: better.
- **Agħar**: worse.
- **Aktar**: more.
- **Aktarx**: likely, probably.
- **Iżjed**: more.
- **Inqas**: less.
- **Biżżejjed**: enough (*with more*).
- **Wisq**: too much.

12. Everyday Maltese words

Let's see often-used words and expressions related to common topics.

12.1 Fill in a form
- **Isem**: name.
- **Kunjom**: last name.
- **Indirizz**: address.
- **Telefon**: telephone.
- **Mowbajl**: cell phone.
- **Ittrè**: email.
- **Imejl**: email.
- **Nazzjonalità**: nationality.
- **Pajjiż**: country.
- **Numru**: number.
- **Raġel**: man.
- **Mara**: woman.
- **Tifel**: son.
- **Tifla**: daughter.
- **Ulied**: children.
- **Ġenituri**: parents.

12.2 Weather
- **Xemx**: sun.
- **Xita**: rain.
- **Riħ**: wind.
- **Ragħad**: thunder.
- **Beraq**: lightning.

- **Temp**: weather, climate.
- **Umdita**: humidity.
- **Kesħa**: cold.
- **Sħana**: hot.
- **Sħaba**: cloud.
- **Tempesta**: storm.

- **X'temp hu**: what weather is it?
- **X'temp ħażin**: What a bad weather (*what weather bad*).

12.3 At the doctor
- **Iċ-ċentru tas-saħħa**: health centre, hospital (*the centre of the health*). You can find those around the Maltese island.
- **Saħħa**: health, goodbye.
- **Ras**: head.
- **Tabib**, -a, tobba: doctor.
- **Marid**, -a, morda: sick.
- **Marda**: disease.
- **Ħalq**: mouth.
- **Sieq**: foot.
- **Riġel**: leg.
- **Ras**: head.
- **Arm**: driegħ.
- **Ambulanza**: ambulance.

12.4 Money & at the shop
- **Daqs**, -ijiet: size.
- **Fluss**: money.

- **Prezz**: price.
- **Ndaqs**: same size.
- **Daqshekk**: of a particular size. Also means: enough.
- **Bqija**: change.

- **Għandek…** : do you have…
- **Irrid nixtri…**: I want to buy (*I want I buy*).

- **Bajd**: eggs.
- **Tuffieħ**: apple.
- **Larinġ**: orange.
- **Tadam**: tomato.
- **Basla**: onion.
- **Karrotti**: carrots.
- **Ġobon**: cheese.
- **Perżut**: ham.
- **Ħobż**: bread.
- **Insalata**: salad.
- **Torta**: pie.
- **Ħalib**: milk.
- **Frott**: fruit.
- **Lanġasa**: pear.
- **Frawli**: strawberries.
- **Ħaxix**: vegetables.
- **Patata**: potato.
- **Ħjara**: cucumber.
- **Ġelat**, -i: ice cream.

- **Ħwejjeġ**: clothes.
- **Ċinturin**: belt.
- **Nuċċali tax-xemx**: sunglasses (*glasses of the sun*).
- **Kappell**: hat.
- **Dettalji**: details.
- **Kuluri oħra**: other colours.
- **Sigaretti**: cigarettes.
- **Televixin, -s**: television.
- **Ktieb**, kotba: book.
- **Gass**: gas.

12.5 Home

- **Flett**: flat.
- **Dar**: house, home.
- **Raħal**: village.
- **Belt**: city. Il-Belt with capital is Valletta.
- **Ġar**, ġirien: neighbour.
- **Kera**: rent.

- **Kamra**: room.
- **Salott**: dining room.
- **Kċina**: kitchen.
- **Kamra tas-sodda**: bedroom (*room of the bed*).
- **Kamra tal-banju**: bathroom (*room of the bath*).
- **Pixxina**: swimming pool.
- **Ġnien**: garden.

- **Sular**: floor.

- **Bejt**: roof.
- **Ħajt**: wall.
- **Bieb**: door.
- **Tieqa**: window.

- **Tapit**: rug, carpet.
- **Forn**: oven.
- **Armarju**: cupboard.
- **Sufan**: couch.
- **Mejda**: table.
- **Sodda**: bed.
- **Purtiera**: curtain.
- **Siġġu**: chair.
- **Lampa**: lamp.
- **Mitraħ**: mattress.
- **Mera**: mirror.
- **Xugaman**: towel.
- **Sapuna**: soap.
- **Xawer**: shower.

12.6: Restaurant

- **Ilma**: water.
- **Nbid**: wine.
- **Kafè**: coffee.

- **Laħam**: meat.
- **Bżar**: pepper.
- **Melħ**: salt.

- **Għaġin**: pasta.
- **Ħut**: fish.
- **Zalzet**: sausages.
- **Ħaruf**: lamb.
- **Majjal**: pork.
- **Butir**: butter.

- **Furketta**: fork.
- **Mgħarfa**: spoon.
- **Tazza**: glass.
- **Sikkina**: knife.
- **Sarvetta**: napkin.
- **Platt**: plate.
- **Flixkun**: bottle.

- **Riħa**: smell, stench.
- **Frisk**, -a, -i: fresh.

- **L-ikla t-tajba**: have a nice meal (*the meal the good*).
- **Għandi l-għatx**: I'm thirsty (*I have the thirst*).
- **Għandi l-ġuħ**: I'm hungry (*I have the hunger*).
- **Jiena bil-ġuħ**: I'm hungry (*I am with hunger*).
- **M'għandix aptit**: I'm not hungry. However, also used as: I don't want to… It doesn't need to be related to food.

12.7 Transport
- **Tal-linja**: bus (*of the line*).
- **Karozza tal-linja**: bus (*car of the line*).
- **Xarabank**: bus.

- **Karozza**: car.
- **Ajruplan**: plane.
- **Vjaġġ**, -i: journey, trip.

12.8 Time

- **Illum**: today.
- **Ilbieraħ**: yesterday.
- **Għada**: tomorrow.
- **Pitgħada**: the day after tomorrow.
- **Ilbieraħ tlura**: the day before yesterday.

- **Sena**: year.
- **Xahar**: month.
- **Ġimgħa**: week. Same as Friday.
- **Minuta**: minute.
- **Siegħa**: hour.
- **Mument**: moment.
- **Jum**: day.
- **Jum ta' negozju**: business day (*day of business*).
- **Nhar**: day.
- **Dakinhar**: on that day.

- **Ħadd**: Sunday.
- **Tnejn**: Monday.
- **Tlieta**: Tuesday.
- **Erbgħa**: Wednesday.
- **Ħamis**: Thursday.
- **Ġimgħa**: Friday.
- **Sibt**: Saturday.

- **Jannar**: January.
- **Frar**: February.
- **Marzu**: March.
- **April**: April.
- **Mejju**: May.
- **Ġunju**: June.
- **Lulju**: July.
- **Awissu**: August.
- **Settembru**: September.
- **Ottobru**: October.
- **Novembru**: November.
- **Diċembru**: December.

- **Sajf**: summer.
- **Ħarifa**: autumn.
- **Xitwa**: winter.
- **Rebbiegħa**: spring.

13. Extra useful phrases

In this chapter, let's see another list of useful phrases, expressions and words for over the phone, to give compliments, to use at a party and others.

13.1 On the phone

- **Għidli**: tell me.
- **Kompli**: continue, go on.
- **Min qed jitkellem?**: Who is it? (*who is speaking*).
- **Inċempel iktar tard**: I'll call later (*I call more late*).
- **In-numru tiegħi hu**: my number is (*the number of mine is*).
- **Żommha**: wait a bit (*keep her*).
- **Messaġġ**: message.

13.2 Compliments

- **Xi ġmiel**: how beautiful (*what beauty*).
- **Inħobbok**: I love you.
- **Qalbi**: my love (*my heart*).
- **Naħseb fik**: I think about you (*I think in you*).
- **Pupa**: beauty (*doll*). Only to use with women.
- **Kemm inti ħelu/ħelwa**: you're very sweet (*how much you are sweet*).
- **Inti għarus?**: Are you in a relationship? (*are you a boyfriend*).
- **Inti għarusa?**: Are you in a relationship? (*are you a girlfriend*).
- **Ħanini**: my sweet, darling. Pet name.
- **Inti anġlu**: you're an angel.

13.3 Party at friend's place

- **Ħu pjaċir**: have fun (*take pleasure*). Shortened as hp.
- **Ħudu pjaċir**. have fun (*take pleasure*). In the plural.
- **Ħu gost / ħudu gost**: have fun (*take pleasure*).
- **Ħu ħsieb /ħudu ħsieb**: take care (*take thought*).
- **Ħu paċenzja /ħudu paċenzja**: be patient (*take patience*).
- **Sieħeb**: friend.
- **Sieħbi**: my friend.
- **Ħabib**, -a, ħbieb: friend.
- **Xbin**: friend.
- **Prosit**: congratulations.
- **Nifraħlek**: congratulations (*I congratulate you*).
- **Awguri**!: Good luck!
- **Taf...**?: Do you know...?
- **Fejn hi rasek**: long time I haven't seen you (*where is your head*).

13.4 Others

- **... waħda ...wieħed** (one) ... **wħud** (some): If one wants to say one day, one says: **jum wieħed**.
- **Waħdi, -ek** ...: alone. (uses attached pronouns)
- **Wieħed wara l-ieħor**: one after the other.
- **Darba waħda**: once (*time one*).
- **Darbtejn**: twice (*time two*).
- **Darb'oħra**: another time, again.

- **Għadni, għadek…**: still. (uses attached pronouns)
- **Ilni, ilek**: since. In combination with verb. (uses attached pronouns)
- **Lest**, -a, -i: ready.
- **Ieħor**, oħra, oħrajn: other.
- **Magħruf, -a, -in**: known.
- **Importanti**: important.
- **Ċert**, -a, -i: sure, certain.
- **Bravu**, -a, -i: clever.

- **Dejjaqtni**: you made me angry (*you narrowed me*).
- **Tant ieħor**: same to you (*so much other*).
- **Fuq kollox**: above all.
- **U l-bqija**: etc…
- **Il-ħin sar**: it is late (*the time became*).
- **Bla dubju**: no doubt (*without doubt*).

- **Ruħ**, erwieħ: soul, people.
- **Bniedem**, bnedim: people.
- **Nies**: people.
- **Periklu**: danger.
- **Problema**, -i: problem.
- **Biċċa**: a piece.
- **Appuntament**: appointment.
- **Deċiżjoni**: decision.
- **Koxxa**: box.
- **Xogħol**: work.
- **Uffiċċju**: office.

- **Parti**, -jiet: part.
- **Ritratt**, -i: picture, photo.
- **Logħba**, -iet: game.
- **Realtà**: reality.
- **Aħbarijiet**: news.
- **Affarijiet**: affairs.
- **Pjan**: plan.
- **Sitwazzjoni**: situation.
- **Verità**: truth.
- **Għajnuna**: help.
- **Battikata**: hassle.

- **Forsi**: maybe.
- **Xorta**: still, same.
- **Pereżempju**: for example.
- **Lura**: back.
- **Kważi**: almost.
- **Ċar**: clear.

- **Finalment**: finally.
- **Normalment**: normally.
- **Onestament**: honestly.
- **Ċertament**: surely.
- **Kompletament**: completely.
- **Soltu**: usually.
- **Is-soltu**: the usual.
- **Tas-soltu**: usual.
- **Bħas-soltu**: as usual.

14. Fun extras

1) Can you understand the meaning of the following sentence? Ċukkulata means chocolate.

"Hawn tad-doughnuts, tajbin! Ara x' għandna llum, tajbin! Ċukkulata, jam, tajbin. Hawn tad-doughnuts, hawn..."[1]

2) Do you understand this typically Maltese phrase?[2]
Hint: something that moves in the picture.

Move back please!

---

[1] Doughnuts for sale. Look what doughnuts we have today. With chocolate and jam. Doughnuts for sale.
Literally: Here's of doughnuts, good! Look what we have today, good! Chocolate, jam, good! Here's of doughnuts, here...

[2] Because Maltese buses can easily be packed, the drivers sometimes repeatedly have to ask to move back into the bus.

15. Learn more Maltese

If you want to learn more Maltese, check out my other books, courses and extra resources via the links below:

Maltese online course: https://bit.ly/3WeVX3G

Maltese basic grammar:

100+ Maltese verbs explained:

More books to learn Maltese:
https://learn-any-language-with-alain.com/product-category/maltese/

More Maltese on: https://learn-any-language-with-alain.com/maltese/

16. The final word - About the author

We're at the end of the book - congratulations, you're much better prepared to learn Maltese.

Curiously, when Alain de Raymond was young, many language teachers told him he wasn't so good at languages. His Dutch was poor. His English teacher even advised him to follow extra courses.

He discovered he loved languages when he went to Germany in 2010. He had some basic German skills but started to speak in German from day one. What he got in return was amazing: friendship, love, respect and a good level of German. Since then, he's passionate about languages.

Now he's proud to be able to express himself in French, Dutch, English, German, Maltese and Spanish. He also has some Portuguese notions. And he's always busy learning new languages and taught some of his languages via tutoring.

He also has a life besides languages. He loves economics, politics and all the processes that shape society. He worked in communications a few years and holds 3 degrees: in Journalism, EU Studies and Management.

Pictures taken from pixabay.com, except in the last two chapters: © Alain de Raymond.

Made in the USA
Las Vegas, NV
25 June 2024